BEYOND WORDS

UNDERSTANDING THE UNSPOKEN LANGUAGE OF THE MIND

ANUSHKA SAHU

Made with ♥ on the Notion Press Platform
www.notionpress.com

For everyone who's ever felt like they were the only one
who felt too much.
You're not alone.

Contents

Foreword

We often measure strength by what is loud and visible. But some of the most powerful things happen quietly—beyond words. This book is about those silent forces inside us: the deep thoughts, the careful observations, and the feelings that don't always get spoken but shape how we see the world and connect with others.

Beyond Words is for anyone who has ever felt more than they could say, who listens when others talk, and who understands without needing to explain. It's about recognizing and honoring the quiet strength that too often goes unnoticed.

In these pages, you'll find ideas and reflections to help you see the value in your own silence and the silent gifts others carry. Whether you're naturally quiet, sensitive, or just curious about what lies beneath the surface, this book aims to bring those hidden parts into the light.

Thank you for reading. I hope Beyond Words offers you insight, comfort, and a new way to appreciate the quiet power inside us all.

Acknowledgements

Writing Beyond Words has been a journey of reflection and discovery, and it wouldn't have been possible without the quiet support of many people.

First, I want to thank my family. Your patience and encouragement, even when I kept to myself, helped me find the courage to share these ideas. Sometimes the loudest support comes from silent understanding, and I'm grateful for that.

To my friends, thank you for being there in your own gentle ways. Whether through a smile, a listening ear, or a quiet moment of shared understanding, you reminded me that connection doesn't always need words.

I am also grateful to the many people—sometimes strangers—who inspired this book by simply being themselves. The thoughtful, the sensitive, and the observers who see the world differently. You showed me the power of listening and feeling beyond what is said.

Thank you to the readers who will hold this book. Your willingness to explore the quiet strengths in yourself and others means a lot. I hope this book offers you comfort, insight, and a reminder that your unspoken gifts matter.

Finally, I want to acknowledge the moments of silence, reflection, and stillness that allowed these ideas to come to life. Sometimes, the most important conversations happen beyond words.

— Anushka Sahu

Preface

This book started as a simple idea: that not all strengths are loud or obvious. Many of us have parts of ourselves that stay quiet—our thoughts, feelings, and ways of understanding the world. These hidden gifts often go unnoticed, even by ourselves.

I wrote Beyond Words because I wanted to explore those silent parts. What does it mean to have a quiet strength? How can we better understand ourselves and others when so much happens beneath the surface?

Throughout this book, you'll find reflections and ideas about the power of listening, feeling deeply, and noticing what isn't said. It's meant for anyone who has ever felt like they don't quite fit the loudness of the world or who wonders if their quiet ways matter.

This isn't a book of quick answers or big declarations. It's a guide to recognizing and appreciating the small, often hidden ways we connect and grow. I hope it helps you find value in your own silence and the silences around you.

Thank you for joining me in this journey beyond words.
— **Anushka Sahu**

I

The Hidden Gift

Have you ever had a moment when you just *knew* how someone was feeling — even though they didn't say a word? Maybe a friend smiled, but their eyes looked sad. Or someone said everything was fine, but you sensed tension underneath. That moment of understanding—when you pick up on feelings hidden beneath the surface—is what I call the **Hidden Gift.**

The Hidden Gift isn't magic or something only a few people have. It's a skill, and like any skill, it can be learned and improved.

This chapter will guide you through how to get started with the Hidden Gift: how to notice the subtle clues people give, how to listen beyond words, and how to train yourself to understand others more deeply, A few things can be-

Pay Attention to Silent Signals

People communicate a lot without words. Their body language, facial expressions, and tone of voice can reveal what they really feel.

For example:

- Someone might say, "I'm fine," but their shoulders are slumped and their voice is soft.
- Eye contact, or the lack of it, often tells a story—avoiding your gaze might mean discomfort or hiding something.

To start developing your Hidden Gift, begin by noticing these silent signals in everyday conversations. Watch how people move, listen to how they speak, and observe how their emotions show up physically.

Learn to Listen Beyond Words

Words are important, but they don't always tell the whole truth. Sometimes people hide their feelings out of fear, pride, or uncertainty.

Instead of just hearing what is said, try to listen to what is not said. If someone changes the subject quickly or gives short answers, it might mean they don't want to open up yet. Respecting that space is also part of understanding.

Ask Questions That Invite Honesty

Curiosity is your friend. When you ask open-ended questions, you give others the chance to share more honestly.

Instead of a simple "How are you?", try asking:

- *"What's been on your mind lately?"*
- *"How are you really feeling about that?"*
- *"Can you tell me more about what happened?"*

These kinds of questions encourage deeper conversations and help you practice reading the hidden feelings behind the words.

Observe Yourself to Understand Others

One of the most important keys to understanding others is learning to observe yourself first. Notice your own feelings, reactions, and body language in different situations. How do you respond when you feel happy, nervous, or upset?

Why does this help? Because our own emotions often serve as a mirror for understanding others. When you recognize a feeling in yourself, it becomes easier to identify it in someone else—even if they express it differently.

For example, if you notice your heart racing when you're anxious, you might recognize the same signs in a friend who seems restless but hasn't said anything.

Self-awareness builds empathy and sharpens your ability to read silent signals in others.

Practice Empathy, Not Judgment

The Hidden Gift is about connecting, not fixing. When you sense someone's feelings, try to imagine their experience without judging it.

You don't need to solve their problems or give advice unless they ask. Sometimes, just being there and understanding is enough.

Reflect and Learn From Experience

After talking with someone, take a moment to reflect:

- What clues did you notice?
- Did their words match their body language?
- How did their feelings make you feel?

Reflection helps sharpen your skill over time. You'll start to notice patterns and get better at understanding people.

Be Patient with Yourself

Developing the Hidden Gift takes time and practice. You won't get it right every time, and that's okay.

Every conversation is an opportunity to learn. The more you pay attention and care, the stronger your gift becomes.

Starting your journey with the Hidden Gift means slowing down, paying close attention, and opening your heart to what others might be feeling beneath the surface. It's a powerful skill that can improve your relationships and deepen your understanding of the people around you.

II
Understanding Silent Signals

Having the Hidden Gift—the ability to understand unspoken feelings—can be powerful. But it can also feel overwhelming if you don't know how to manage it. When you constantly sense others' emotions, it's easy to get drained, confused, or even lose your own sense of self.

This chapter is about how to manage your Hidden Gift with care and respect—both for others and for yourself. Here's a few things you can do to manage it well-

Know Your Limits

Just like any skill, your ability to read people's feelings has limits. You can't always understand everything, and you can't always fix every problem you sense. Accepting this is the first step to managing the gift.

Set boundaries on how much emotional energy you give. It's okay to take breaks, especially when you feel overwhelmed or tired.

Protect Your Own Emotions

When you feel others' emotions deeply, it can affect your own mood. Learn to check in with yourself regularly. Ask:

- How do I feel right now?
- Are these feelings mine or someone else's?
- What do I need to feel balanced again?

Here are some tips to protect your emotional health:

Take time for yourself: Spend a few minutes daily doing something calming, like breathing exercises or listening to music.

- *Use visualization:* Imagine a protective bubble around you that keeps negative emotions from affecting your core.
- *Journal your feelings:* Writing helps separate your own emotions from those you sense in others.
- *Practice saying no:* It's okay to decline emotional support sometimes, especially if you feel drained.
- *Connect with nature:* A walk outside or time in fresh air can reset your emotional energy.

Don't Take It Personally

Sometimes, you might sense negative feelings or judgments that aren't about you—they belong to someone else's struggles or fears.

Remember, understanding someone's feelings doesn't mean you have to carry their burdens. You can be compassionate without absorbing their pain.

Choose When to Share

Your gift gives you insights others might not see. But sharing these insights takes care.

Not everyone is ready or willing to hear the feelings you sense beneath the surface. Before speaking up, consider:

- "Is this the right time and place?"
- "Will this help or hurt?"
- "How can I share gently and respectfully?'

Sometimes, just listening quietly is the most supportive choice.

Keep Learning and Practicing

Managing the Hidden Gift is a continuous journey. As you practice, you'll learn more about yourself and others.

Try reflecting regularly: What worked well in your interactions? When did you feel overwhelmed? How can you improve your balance next time?

Use Your Gift for Good

When managed well, your Hidden Gift becomes a powerful tool for kindness and connection. Use it to support friends, understand conflicts, and create deeper relationships.

But always remember: your own well-being comes first. Caring for yourself is the foundation for truly caring for others.

Managing the Hidden Gift means knowing your limits, protecting your heart, and choosing your actions wisely.

With patience and practice, you'll find the balance that lets you use this special skill in a healthy, helpful way.

III

Growing the Gift

Having the Hidden Gift is just the beginning. The real strength comes from learning how to use it wisely — to grow, improve, and understand both yourself and others more deeply.

Learning from the Hidden Gift means paying attention, reflecting on your experiences, and practicing new ways to sharpen your insight. Here's a few things I suggest-

Observe Yourself to Understand Others

The best way to understand others is to start by observing yourself. Notice your own feelings, reactions, and patterns. When you become aware of your inner world, you build a clearer lens to see what others might be feeling.

Ask yourself questions like:

- *"What am I feeling right now?"*
- *"How do I react when someone is upset?"*
- *'What clues do I pick up without realizing it?"*

This self-awareness is the foundation for learning from your gift.

<u>Reflect on Your Experiences</u>

After conversations or social situations, take a moment to think back on what you noticed.

1. *What feelings did you sense?*
2. *Were you right or wrong?*
3. *How did your feelings influence your understanding?*

Reflection helps you recognize patterns and improve your ability to interpret silent signals.

<u>Learn from Mistakes</u>

Nobody's perfect. Sometimes you might misunderstand or misread a situation. Instead of getting discouraged, use these moments as lessons.

Ask yourself:

- *What made me misinterpret this?*
- *What could I do differently next time?*

Mistakes are valuable feedback for growth.

Practice Empathy Every Day

Empathy isn't just feeling sorry for someone; it's stepping into their shoes and trying to see the world through their eyes.

Try simple exercises like imagining a friend's struggles or joys, and ask how you would feel in their place. This strengthens your emotional connection and sharpens your gift.

<u>Stay Curious and Open</u>

The world of emotions is complex and ever-changing. Stay curious about people and their stories. Ask questions, listen deeply, and remain open to new perspectives.

Your gift grows when you embrace learning as a lifelong journey.

Use Your Gift with Purpose

As you learn, decide how you want to use your gift. Whether it's helping friends, resolving conflicts, or simply being a better listener, let your purpose guide your growth.

Learning is *not* just about skill, but about meaningful connection.

Learning from the Hidden Gift means staying mindful, reflective, and open. With time, patience, and practice, your ability to understand others will become a powerful source of compassion and connection.

IV
Behind the Masks

Have you ever noticed how people often act differently around others than how they truly feel inside? This is what we call wearing *masks* — hiding our real emotions to fit in, protect ourselves, or avoid judgment.

Understanding why we wear masks helps us see both ourselves and others more clearly. It also deepens the Hidden Gift, because reading beyond the mask reveals the real feelings beneath.

Why Do We Wear Masks?

There are many reasons why people hide their true feelings:

- *Fear of Rejection:* We worry that if others see our vulnerabilities, they might reject or judge us.
- *Social Expectations:* Society often expects us to behave in certain "acceptable" ways, even if they don't match our feelings.
- *Protecting Others:* Sometimes, we hide feelings to avoid hurting or worrying people we care about.

- *Personal Insecurity:* We may feel our true emotions aren't valid or acceptable, so we put on a mask instead.

Wearing masks is a natural survival skill, but it can make real connection harder.

How to Spot the Mask

Your Hidden Gift helps you notice when someone is hiding their feelings. Look for clues like:

- Body language that doesn't match their words (a smile that doesn't reach the eyes).
- Sudden changes in tone or pace when talking about certain topics.
- Avoiding eye contact or changing the subject quickly.
- Small signs of discomfort or nervousness.

These signs can be the cracks where the real emotions peek through.

Why Wearing Masks Can Be Harmful

While masks protect us, they can also create distance:

- They block honest communication.
- They cause misunderstandings.
- They increase feelings of loneliness and isolation.
- They make it harder to trust ourselves and others.

Recognizing masks is the first step toward breaking down these walls.

Tips to Gently Unmask Yourself or Others

1. Build Trust Gradually
People need to feel safe before they take off their masks. Show consistent kindness, respect, and patience.

2. Share Your Own Feelings
Model openness by sharing your emotions in small, honest ways. This encourages others to do the same.

3. Listen Without Judgment
Create a space where others can speak freely without fear of criticism.

4. Be Patient
Removing a mask is scary. Give people time and space to open up at their own pace.

<u>Using the Hidden Gift Respectfully</u>

Your ability to see past the mask is a gift, but it comes with responsibility. Use your insight to support, not expose or pressure others.

Respect privacy and only explore deeper feelings when it feels safe and appropriate.

Wearing masks is a part of human nature, but recognizing and understanding them can lead to more authentic relationships. The Hidden Gift helps you look beyond appearances to the heart of what people feel.

V
The Power of Listening

Some people hear.
Some people listen.
And a few—very few—*really* listen.

We often think helping someone means giving advice, saying something wise, or knowing the perfect thing to say. But sometimes, the most powerful thing you can do is to say... nothing.

Just listen.

Listening Is More Than Staying Quiet

You might think, *"I don't interrupt, I'm a good listener."* But real listening isn't just about staying silent. It's about being present.

It means:

- Not planning what you'll say next.

- Not mentally solving their problem.
- Not secretly waiting for your turn to speak.

It's about letting their words exist without trying to fix them.

The Hidden Gift in Action

If you have the Hidden Gift, you can usually sense when someone is saying less than they feel. That's when listening becomes more than just a skill—it becomes an act of care.

You start noticing:

- The pause before they speak.
- The forced smile.
- The way their voice shakes a little.

And instead of jumping in, you *stay*. You let them know:

"You don't have to be okay right now. I'm not going anywhere."

Sometimes, that's all they need to say what they've been holding back.

Why Listening Feels So Rare

People aren't used to being listened to.
They're used to being:

- Interrupted.
- Rushed.
- Dismissed.
- Told what they "should" do.

So when someone actually listens—*really listens*—it almost feels magical.

That moment when someone says,

"Wow... I've never said that out loud before,"

is a sign you've given them something powerful: **"space"**.

You Don't Have to Understand Everything

Here's the truth: you don't need to fully "get it" to be a good listener.

You don't need to have gone through what they're going through.

You just need to be willing to understand what it *feels* like.

You don't need to relate.

You just need to care.

Listening Heals in Small Ways

When someone is falling apart, your quiet attention can be the thing that holds them together. Not your words. Not your solutions.

Just your **presence.**

Let them talk. Let them cry. Let them ramble. Let them sit in silence if they need to.

And when they're done, don't rush to respond.

Just let your listening speak for itself.

The Power Isn't in What You Say

The power is in how you make them feel:

- Safe.
- Seen.
- Unjudged.

That's what listening does.

That's what the Hidden Gift is really about.

So the next time you think, *"I don't know what to say,"* remember: maybe you don't need to say anything.

Just *listen.*

That might be the most powerful thing you can give.

VI

Breaking the Silence

Silence isn't always empty. Sometimes, it's full of things that were never said out loud.

We've all been there—sitting with someone, feeling like there's something unspoken hanging in the air. Maybe it's a shift in their mood. Maybe it's something they didn't finish saying. Or maybe... it's you. You've been holding back, rehearsing your words in your head but not letting them leave your mouth.

Silence can be safety. But it can also be a prison.

Why People Don't Speak

People stay silent for a hundred reasons:

- They're afraid of being judged.
- They don't want to burden anyone.
- They don't know how to say it right.

• They think it won't matter.

And sometimes, they don't even know what's wrong—just that saying it out loud would make it real.

For those with the Hidden Gift, silence doesn't feel neutral. It feels loud. You can sense the tension behind someone's smile, the meaning behind their shrug, the things they almost—but didn't—say.

But the gift isn't just about noticing silence.

It's about knowing **when** and **how** to gently break it.

Not Every Silence Needs to Be Filled

Let's clear this up: not all silence is bad. Some silences are peaceful, comfortable. They're the kind of quiet that says, *"I feel safe with you. I don't need to perform."*

But there's another kind. The kind where someone is aching to speak but too scared to try. Where words build up like pressure in a bottle. That kind of silence doesn't just fade—it *weighs*.

Sometimes, being the person who breaks that silence is the kindest thing you can do. But it's not about throwing questions or forcing confessions. It's about offering a crack of light.

Like saying:

"You don't have to explain, but I'm here if you want to."

That one sentence can make someone feel less alone.

The First Word is the Hardest

Breaking silence—especially your *own*—takes courage.

Think of how many times you've wanted to speak up but didn't:

- You stayed quiet in class even when you knew the answer.
- You nodded and smiled when a joke hurt your feelings.
- You said "I'm fine" when you weren't.

Sometimes we stay silent because speaking feels like admitting weakness. But in reality, breaking silence is a sign of strength. It means you're letting truth into the room. Even if your voice shakes. Even if the words come out messy.

And sometimes, the one with the Hidden Gift needs to be the one to go first.

"I've been feeling a little off lately. Have you?"

That small act of vulnerability gives others permission to be honest too.

How to Break the Right Kind of Silence

There's a difference between breaking silence and breaking boundaries. You're not trying to unlock someone. You're letting them know the door is open.

Here are a few quiet ways to do it:

- **Make space**: Sit beside someone. Let the silence breathe a little. Then say something soft like, *"You've been quiet lately—want to talk about it?"*
- **Offer safety:** Say, *"Whatever you're feeling, I'm not here to fix it—I'm just here."*
- **Be honest first:** Share something small from your own life. Vulnerability is contagious in the best way.
- **Ask once, not twice:** If someone isn't ready, don't press. Your patience speaks louder than repeated questions.

When Silence is the Sound of Healing

Sometimes, silence isn't a wall—it's a blanket.

After someone opens up, don't rush to fill the space with advice or analysis. Let it sit. Let the quiet hold them. Let them breathe in the relief of being heard.

There's a special kind of silence that follows honesty—a soft, shared stillness that says, "That was real."

If you've ever had that moment, you know how powerful it is.

If you haven't, maybe you'll be the one to create it.

Your Presence is the Break

You don't need the perfect words to help someone speak. You just need to be *there*—calm, open, and *real*.

People break their own silences when they feel safe.

And safety doesn't come from pressure.

It comes from presence.

So the next time someone goes quiet, don't rush to fix it. Don't rush to fill it.

Sit with them. Wait with them.

And when the moment feels right, offer the softest nudge:

"You don't have to talk. But if you do... I'll listen."

That's how silence begins to break.

That's how people begin to heal.

VII
Trust and Truth

Trust isn't given freely—it's *earned*. And one of the strongest ways to earn trust is through truth. Being truthful isn't just about avoiding lies; it's about showing honesty in how you think, feel, and act.

Why Truth Builds Trust

When you're honest, you create a safe space for others. They know what to expect from you. Your words and actions match, and that consistency feels reliable.

For someone with the Hidden Gift, this matters even more. You notice when things don't add up. Truthfulness helps bridge that gap and invites others to be real with you.

How to Win Trust with Truth

- **Be Open About Your Feelings:**Share what's really on your mind, even when it's uncomfortable. Saying, "I'm feeling nervous about this" or "I don't know the answer" shows you're human, not perfect. People trust realness more than perfection.

- **Admit Mistakes**: Nobody's perfect. Owning up when you mess up shows integrity. It's better than hiding or blaming others, which breaks trust fast.
- **Speak Clearly and Simply**: Avoid sugarcoating or beating around the bush. Clear, honest communication helps others understand you better and reduces confusion.
- **Follow Through on Your Words**: Truth isn't just what you say but what you do. Keep promises and be dependable.
- **Be Consistent:** Truth builds trust when it's steady. Don't change your story or behavior to fit the moment. Consistency shows you're reliable.
- **Respect Others's Truths:** Encourage honesty from others by accepting their feelings, even if you don't agree. Trust grows when people feel heard, not judged.

What If Truth Hurts?

Sometimes truth can sting. It might reveal hard feelings or mistakes. But trust grows stronger when truth is shared gently and respectfully.

Try saying things like:

- "I want to be honest because I respect you."
- "This is hard to say, but I think it's important."
- "I'm sharing this so we can understand each other better."

Truth Creates a Two-Way Street
Winning trust isn't only about your truth—it's about welcoming others' truths too. Listen carefully and show

empathy. When people feel safe being honest, trust grows naturally.

Trust Yourself by Being True

Your gift lets you sense when something feels off. Use your truth to guide how much trust to give and when to ask for more honesty.

Truth isn't always easy, but it's the strongest tool you have to win and keep trust. When you choose truth, you build connections that are real, lasting, and meaningful.

Quick Tips: How to Win Trust Using Truth

- **Start with honesty:** Share your true feelings first, even if it's just a little. It encourages others to open up.
- **Be patient:** Trust takes time. Let others share when they're ready.
- **Use gentle honesty:** Speak your truth kindly, not harshly.
- **Show you care:** Explain why you're being honest — because you value the relationship.
- **Listen without judgment:** When others share, accept their truth without criticizing.
- **Follow through:** Do what you say to prove your honesty is real.
- **Trust your instincts:** Your Hidden Gift helps you sense when to ask more or when to give space.

VIII
Emotional Cluelessness

Have you ever felt like everyone else just gets feelings... except you? Like emotions are a secret code you can't crack?

You're not alone. Emotional cluelessness happens more than you think.

What Is Emotional Cluelessness?

It means having trouble recognizing or understanding your own or others' emotions. You might feel something strong but can't name it. Or notice someone's vibe but can't tell if they're upset, tired, or just distracted.

This makes social moments confusing. You might misread reactions, miss subtle cues, or feel overwhelmed by feelings you don't understand.

Why Does It Happen?

Emotions are messy. Sometimes we weren't taught how to talk about them. And if you have the Hidden Gift, you might sense emotions all around but struggle to sort them out.

The Hidden Gift and Emotional Cluelessness

It's like hearing pieces of a conversation but missing the full story. You sense tension or sadness but don't know why.

Instead of ignoring this, try to get curious: "What's really going on here?"

How to Handle Emotionally Clueless People

Dealing with people who don't understand emotions can be frustrating.

Here's how to make it easier:

- **Be clear**: Don't expect them to "*just* get it." Use simple words to explain your feelings.
- **Give examples**: Share specific moments to help them understand.
- **Be patient**: They might need time to catch up or ask questions.
- **Set boundaries**: If their cluelessness hurts you, it's okay to step back or say what you need.
- **Encourage openness**: Invite honest talks instead of guessing games.

Remember, they aren't always trying to be difficult—they just experience emotions differently.

Growing Your Emotional Skills

Try labeling your feelings: "I feel anxious," or "I'm frustrated." Notice body signals—like a tight chest or shaky hands—that hint at emotions.

Ask questions gently: "You seem off today, want to talk?" And be patient with yourself when feelings are confusing.

You're Not Alone

Emotional cluelessness isn't a flaw—it's part of being human. Your Hidden Gift might make understanding emotions tricky, but with time and kindness, you'll get better at it.

Take It One Step at a Time

Next time you feel lost in emotions, remember: it's okay not to have all the answers now.

Be patient with yourself and others. Keep listening and learning. Every step brings you closer to unlocking the Hidden Gift.

IX

Knowing When to Stop

There's a difference between being **intuitive** and being **intrusive.** The Hidden Gift—this quiet superpower of reading people—can be beautiful. But like all powerful things, it needs boundaries. And one of the most underrated skills for those with this gift is knowing when to stop.

Sometimes, the silence isn't an invitation to dig deeper. Sometimes, it's a door slowly closing, and the kindest thing you can do is not to force it *open*.

The Urge to Understand Everything

Let's be honest: it's tempting. When you sense something's wrong with someone—an odd shift in tone, a forced smile, an "I'm fine" that obviously isn't—you want to help. You want to fix it. You want to know. And that's not a bad thing. It means you care.

But pushing too hard, even with the best intentions, can make people feel exposed or pressured. Sometimes people aren't ready to talk. Sometimes they don't have the words. And sometimes they just want to be left alone for a while. That's okay.

Knowing when to stop means knowing when to respect the unknown—even if your intuition is screaming for answers.

People Aren't Puzzles

We often treat people like problems we need to solve. But the truth is, no one likes being treated like a mystery to be cracked. Especially when they're vulnerable.

If you keep pushing someone to open up when they've clearly shut the door, it doesn't make them feel safe—it makes them feel cornered. And when people feel cornered, they either lash out or shut down even more.

Sometimes, the most powerful thing you can do is wait. Give space. Let them know you're there, without trying to prove it.

The Art of the Exit

There's a subtle strength in stepping back gracefully.

Let's say you're talking to a friend who's going through something. You sense they're holding back. You ask once—gently. They say they're fine. You ask again. They shrug. At that point, your instinct might be to push further: "You can tell me anything, you know." But what if instead, you just said:

"No pressure at all. I'm here whenever you feel ready."

That sentence does more than a dozen questions ever could. It tells them: *I see you, I respect your pace, and I'm not going anywhere.*

That's the gift of knowing when to stop.

Stopping Doesn't Mean Giving Up

A lot of people confuse stopping with quitting. "If I stop asking, they'll think I don't care." But that's not how emotional connection works. You don't need to force closeness. You *earn* it—through patience, trust, and presence.

By choosing to stop at the right time, you're saying:

"I value your comfort more than my curiosity."

And that? That's powerful.

A Quick Check-In With Yourself

Here are a few signs you might need to pull back:

- You're asking more questions than they're answering.
- They keep changing the subject.
- Their tone goes from open to distant.
- You feel like you're working too hard to keep the conversation deep.

If you notice those signs, pause. Don't make it awkward. Just gently shift gears. Talk about something lighter. Or simply say, "No worries—want to do something fun instead?"

You're not closing a door. You're just waiting until it opens naturally.

It's Not Just About Conversations

"Knowing when to stop" isn't *just* about other people. It applies to how we treat ourselves, too.

Ever catch yourself overthinking a moment for the tenth time? Replaying something you said? Worrying if you misread someone's tone? That's when you need to stop—not because your thoughts are wrong, but because they've become louder than real life.

Take a breath. Step outside. Do something silly. Let it go for now. Give your mind the same grace you'd give someone else.

The Balance Between Effort and Ease

Here's the truth: You can't always say the perfect thing. You won't always read people right. You're not a mind-reader—you're human.

But what makes your gift shine is the way you hold space for others. And sometimes, holding space means knowing when to step back, not lean in.

So the next time you sense something beneath the surface, remember this:

You don't need to dive in. You just need to be there—patient, present, and quietly waiting.

That's the moment people start to feel safe.
And eventually, they speak.
When they're ready.

X

Setting Boundaries

If you have the Hidden Gift, you probably notice when something feels off—sometimes before others do. But knowing what feels off is just the start. The real challenge? Setting boundaries.

What Are Boundaries?

Boundaries are like invisible fences that protect your feelings, time, and energy. They tell others what's okay and what's not okay with you.

<u>Without boundaries, people might:</u>

- Overstep and take advantage.
- Drain your energy.
- Ignore your needs.

Why Boundaries Matter

People with the Hidden Gift can feel emotions deeply and pick up on others' feelings too. That means if you don't set clear limits, you might absorb too much stress or hurt.

Boundaries help you stay balanced and keep your emotional space safe.

Types of Boundaries

1. **Physical**: How close someone can get to you or what touches are okay.
2. **Emotional**: What feelings you share and how much emotional support you give.
3. **Time**: How much time you spend with people or on tasks.
4. **Digital**: What you share online and how often you respond to messages.

How to Set Boundaries

Know your limits: Pay attention to when you feel uncomfortable, tired, or overwhelmed. Those feelings are clues.

1. **Be clear**: Say what you need in simple words. ("I need some quiet time," or "Please don't raise your voice.")
2. **Practice saying no**: It's okay to say no without explaining yourself.
3. **Stick to your boundaries**: It's normal for people to test limits—stand firm kindly but firmly.
4. **Use "I" statements**: ("I feel overwhelmed when...") This keeps things about your feelings, not blaming others.

What If Someone Pushes Your Boundaries?

It happens. Some people don't notice or respect boundaries right away.

- Remind them calmly.
- Repeat your boundary if needed.
- If they keep pushing, it's okay to step away or limit contact.

Boundaries Are Self-Care

Setting boundaries isn't selfish—it's essential. It helps you:

- Protect your energy.
- Focus on what matters to you.
- Build healthier relationships.

Boundaries and the Hidden Gift

Because you sense so much, boundaries can keep you from feeling overwhelmed. They let you choose what feelings you take in and when to step back.

Practice Makes Perfect

Start small. Try setting one boundary this week—maybe about your time or space. Notice how it feels to say no or ask for what you need.

You might feel nervous at first. That's normal. But every time you protect your space, you get stronger.

Remember

Your feelings matter. Your space matters. Your time matters.

Setting boundaries is a way to respect yourself—and when you do, others will too.

XI

Building Genuine Connections

Having the Hidden Gift means you notice things others might miss—the small shifts in tone, the subtle body language, the unspoken feelings. This ability gives you a powerful advantage: the chance to build truly genuine connections.

But what does *"genuine connection"* really mean? And how can you use your gift to create relationships that last?

What Makes a Connection Genuine?

A genuine connection happens when two people feel seen and understood—not just on the surface, but deep down.

It's when you don't have to pretend or hide your true self. You feel comfortable sharing your thoughts, your fears, and your dreams without fear of judgment.

How Your Gift Helps You Connect

Your Hidden Gift lets you pick up on feelings others might hide, which means you can respond with kindness, patience, and real empathy.

You might sense when someone is feeling left out, anxious, or overwhelmed—even if they don't say a word.

This insight lets you reach out in the right way and at the right time, making people feel noticed and valued.

Tips for Building Genuine Connections

- **Talk About Their Interests:** People love to share what they care about. Use your gift to notice what excites them and bring it up in conversation. Showing genuine interest makes them feel valued and understood.
- **Think Before You Speak:** Because you notice so much, it's important to pause and choose your words carefully. Think about how what you say might be received, and try to communicate in a way that respects their feelings.
- **Adapt Your Personality:** Sometimes, adjusting how you act or respond to match the other person's style can help build rapport. It doesn't mean being fake—just finding common ground and making them feel comfortable around you.
- **Be Present and Listen:** Even while adapting, stay truly engaged. People can tell when you're genuinely paying attention versus just trying to impress.
- **Follow Up and Show You Care:** Building connection is ongoing. Check in, remember details, and show you care beyond just one interaction.

When It Feels Hard to Connect

Sometimes your gift can make connections feel overwhelming. You might absorb others' emotions or worry about reading too much into things.

Remember:

- It's okay to take breaks and recharge.
- Boundaries protect your well-being and keep relationships healthy.
- Not every connection has to be deep—sometimes, light and easy interactions are just as important.

The Reward of Genuine Connection

Building real connections isn't always easy, but it's worth it.

When you connect deeply, you create friendships and bonds that support and uplift you. You feel understood, accepted, and less alone.

Your Hidden Gift isn't just about noticing what's hidden — it's about using that awareness to build bridges between hearts.